About the author

Denzel Eboji was born in July 2004 and lives in Dagenham, Essex. He was born to parents Angela Idi Eboji and Eugene Eboji. He has a brother; Darmani.

He goes to Abbs Cross Performing Arts Academy and is in year 9.

Email:eboji101@yahoo.co.uk

2

Praises for Denzel's journey...

Denzel is a talented actor and full of life on stage but off stage, he is incredibly down to earth. He shows such enthusiasm and professionalism when acting. We are proud of him and his achievements...

Agatha - Aunt

Denzel started the Academy at a young age and although fairly shy at this stage, I very early on noticed that he had something special and would do well in performing arts. After securing his first professional role playing young Simba in Lion King, Denzel's confidence and performance skills just went from strength to strength. Watching his journey so far has been amazing. Both on and off stage Denzel has proved to be a true professional and I am sure he has a very bright future ahead of him.

Claire - Agent

I taught Denzel in year 3 and he was shy. Then one day I heard that he was performing in the West end. So proud of him and watching him succeed has been amazing!!

Mrs Turner – Primary School Teacher

Introduction

I have read several books on miracles and I just never thought or imagined that the past six years of my life would be a miracle. I always got very curious about movies on miracles. When my mum looked at me one day with tears in her eyes and said I was her little miracle and always will be, the first thing that I thought about was the movie "Heaven is for real". I asked her if when I was once in hospital, it was just like in the movie. Mum smiled and said "Son, we all face our own battles as long as we see the hand of God in our situation, whether by breakthrough or consolation. It is our very personal miracle. Once we start comparing, we get our eyes off the miracle worker; God and we forget what a miracle is". I couldn't understand it all well. She went on to joke with me and said, "when you make your own bed properly son, which sure will be a miracle then you will very well understand it". Dad then walked in laughing and said I actually make my own bed well these days as he checks it, but only after ten reminders. Well, I am just not a morning person and it takes an army of Mum and Dad most mornings to get me out of bed. But I guess this is just an excuse because I get up early on Christmas day to open the presents under the Christmas tree. Back to my conversation with mum! She opened a dictionary and picked out what she considered the best definition and changed it. She said, well the dictionary says a miracle is a surprising and welcome event that is not explicable by natural or scientific laws and is therefore considered to be the work of a divine agency. Mum quickly looked at me and said "I am going to change the ending of this sentence with God; a miracle is the work of God Himself. I decided not to argue with her as she sounded so sure, but I really wanted to hear about it, so I quickly said "Oookay mum tell me about this erm work of God on my life. I sure am curious because I am only a boy, how could God have done work on me, I thought to myself."

Mum went on to tell me that a miracle does not only happen over a long period of time. She then paused and asked me if I wanted to hear that from my aunt Rachel, who is her only sister, but knowing how much Aunt Rachel loves to talk, I got anxious that I would not hear the end of this story. We both laughed and mum continued to explain. She said I was born a healthy bouncing baby and weighed 7 pounds. Mum and Dad were so thankful, but because I was their first born, they were so clueless that they even had to wait for my grandmother (Mum's mother) to give me a good bath after I was born. I found that so funny. Grandmother arrived two days after I was brought home from the hospital, all the way from Malawi, Africa. I felt special!!! Mum continued to say that she found the adjusting to having a new born baby okay until the idea of going back to work hit her. She tried to balance job search with looking after me and she struggled. When mum and dad talked about how they were both going to work and afford childcare, the idea of an au pair appeared and Mum found a job and an au pair moved in. They did not have enough knowledge on what to look for in an au pair than the fact that someone needed to watch me. The au pair placed me in front of the Television the whole day and she watched it ninety percent of the time. Mum said she would not blame her, as they did not know better. The au pair left and I had another younger au pair to look after me. By this time Mum and Dad were building their careers for us kids. The au pair did a great job of looking after me.

The Shock

I started primary school and when I was in year 1 my teacher noticed that I did not learn words as quick as other kids and I was slow with my speech. The teacher informed Mum and advised that I should be taken to a Speech Therapist. This came as a total shock to my parents. Questions and anxiety took over their thoughts. Does this mean Denzel will not fully develop in his speech and brain? Did we miss something? Did we do something wrong? How will this affect us? How will we get through this? Will we even get through this? Dad took some time off as it was easier for him than it was for mum, so he immediately started taking me to a Speech Therapist and play groups. Mum on the other hand had a wakeup call that I was not talking to anyone that much hence the delay in speaking. She quickly searched online and found The Academy

Performing Arts School in Barking for me to attend on Sunday afternoon. She thought that was going to help in getting me into conversations. The academy was exciting for me and will always be a place where I discovered another Denzel! One that was not so shy. Mum recalls my first show ever at Queens theatre with the Academy. She said I was so shy. She got a front seat but I came on stage and only moved my shoulders. She was surprised but was so proud of her boy. Aww sweet! By this time I was 8 years old and was taken onto the Academy Agency. Alex started representing me as my agent before Claire took over.

Divine Intervention

I love those people who see talent in you that others do not. Mum calls that a divine connection. A connection that God, in His divinity arranges to either help one person or both. Mum then looked up and said "Son, God looks out for us, He orders our steps, I know some steps may not be fun or nice, but God takes all the things we experience and He works it all out for good." By this time I am worried that this story will end up in a sermon, but I thought I would give Mum a few minutes after all, I needed every detail. She then looked into my eyes and said "Denzel, life does not work out the same for everyone but the bible says that God never puts more on us than we can bear (1 Corinthians 10:13) and that is hard to understand for most people. When I look back at how your Dad and I just got up to

7

improve your speech, even though we had not submitted our lives to Christ fully by that time, God was unconditionally giving us the grace to push forward. We did not see it back then, believe me!" Grace is what made Mum get online to find the Academy. That's Mum's conclusion.

The Academy was such great fun! There were so many of us and neither did Mum and Dad or I picture that I would be performing in West end theatres. Surely, there is a God who enables us to do things that we would not do in our natural realm. Oh yeah! I do believe that. I know this could turn into a long debate because some believe there sure is a God while others could do a teaching in evolution, and others would choose to remain on the fence. In my opinion, I believe that every good thing comes from above (James 1:17) but this book is not to convince you or lead us into a debate, No! My parents always say that we should respect what others believe, but what is important is to protect what we believe. So, back to what enables us to do what we do. Mum continued to give my little inexperienced head some wisdom and she said, "little one, our lives are branches and God is the vine as the Bible says in John 15:5. If we detach our lives from God, it is like when we pluck an apple from the tree. After a while, the apple will start to rot". Mum looked at me and thought I did not understand and went on to say that my kindle is the platform where I am able to re ad my books. If we take away the platform; be it the kindle or my smart phone then I am unable to read a book. I looked at mum and had a thousand arguments on what she said. I could name so many stars who are brilliant on stage or television and do not believe there is a God. These do very well in life and are successful! Mum said"Ooh I am sure you could mention many people that are successful and do not acknowledge God. Yes that is true but those people handle success and challenges very differently from believers."

Then mum said "Ooh, look how we have diverted from our story. Back to the Academy…. "The Academy really helped you to realize that there sure is a gift in you by exposing you to auditions. I never wanted you to be famous, your Dad always said you would be a doctor, mainly because that is what he wanted to be, but it is only fair and our duty as parents is to allow you to use the gift you have as long as it is not destroying your life. We were so thankful for the shows you were in at local theatres and did not push you for anything more and I am glad". I was in two shows which were in Essex and I remember enjoying them so much. When Claire suggested I go for Lion king cub school for three months to get into the West end musical, I thought to myself more fun and more acting. It was one of the greatest three months of my life. Meeting new people and learning a lot of new things. I now believe that if it was not for Claire being used by God, I would not have gotten into the Lion king musical.

Auditions

I did not even know I could sing well till the auditions for Lion King. The queue to the auditions was long and Dad kept on saying "are we going to be seen today? Hey Denzel, you remember the lines right, I know you can do it! Just make sure you work hard in school too!". Although I was nervous, I smiled at Dad in agreement because I knew if I said no, he would get me off the queue. That is how serious Dad is about education and not getting arrogant, thinking; I made it and not work hard in school. When we are at home Mum listens to that and tops it up with God and I end up with a complete sermon from them both! So…back to auditions. The Lion King was one of my many auditions. Previously, I auditioned for the Body Guard and was disappointed when I did not get it. I was in Body Guard School and some kids were cast without us knowing. One day I asked one boy why he had a full script. He proudly said "because I got the part! That did hurt so much. I just thought well, there is the Academy and Claire was ever so lovely to me.I also auditioned for a movie. Mum and I had to take baby Darmani with us all the way to Twickenham. Again I did not make it!!

The prophecy

While I was waiting to hear from Disney to see if I was cast as young Simba in Lion king, my Aunt - Rachel heard a word from God about me. Yes, a prophesy!! She came to mum one evening and said "I do not know if am right or not but I would rather say it than be sorry. God said that Denzel will be amazed, but he needs to know where all these things (meaning the blessings) come from, otherwise the success will destroy him." Mum said she was taken aback by all that was said, she had questions. Was she not being a good mother and not showing her son the way he should go so he should never depart from it? Was she not listening to God or was Aunt Rachel just indirectly correcting her? Thoughts ran through her mind and she really struggled with those words but decided to teach me and my brother more of the Word of God. Mum and Dad took me to cub school each Friday for three months before I was cast as young Simba. I was amazed! Shocked! I had to pinch myself several times. What was even more amazing was that I would be the young Simba at 9 years old! Mum then sat down with me to explain that as James 1 verse 17 says "Every good thing comes from God", my role as young Simba was not just because I was great, there may have been other kids who auditioned better than me, but God allowed that I get the role. I had so many questions, I asked why did God allow me not to get the Body Guard role, but I thought I would leave the debate for another day. My younger brother Darmani quickly asked if God allowed him to fall off his bike and why. Mum then explained that just as they, meaning Mum and Dad do not explain everything they do or allow, God does not as well. But that may sound like he is bullying us until we get to understand God as our heavenly Father. We prayed and gave thanks to God that night and asked Him to help us to keep Him at the centre of everything. I talked a lot with my family.

The journey

Lion King the musical

The experience of being in the Lion King is something that has left a mark of thanks giving on my heart and a great reminder that when we do all that we can, and work hard at it, God will do all that we cannot do. I also learnt that there is a responsibility with every step we climb and the higher we go, the more the responsibility. My time of sitting in front of the television flipping channels was sometimes down to zero and Dad made sure of that. I mean he changed his schedule just to make sure I did my homework. I also had to leave school earlier which meant that I had to catch up with what others were learning in my own time. My parents then decided to get a private tutor who came home every time I had a free evening. She was an American girl with mahogany red hair; I loved her accent so I paid attention. She returned to America after a few months. In preparation for SATS exams I had a lovely home teacher for English who helped me a lot. Then they decided to send me for maths tutoring. I thought ohh noo and I refused! But Mum and Dad would not have it. I had to go for this lesson on a Saturday morning and I am not a morning person. That's no excuse but I used to finish shows late at night and did not go to bed straight away even when the lights were off. Yes Mum and Dad would switch the lights off as soon as I got into bed. I thought that was mean but I now kind of understand. Dad always reminded me and still does remind me how much I need to get education, no matter where I end up, whether it be sports or acting. The private tuitions helped a great deal and I did not fall behind in class. My primary school was very supportive and I will forever be thankful to the Headmistress for supporting my licence applications. The kids in my school year even came to watch me. Each contract was for six months and I loved the other kids I acted with, although not every day was perfect with everyone. I tried to get along with all and during the days when I had an argument with any of the kids, my day was ruined. This was mainly because I thought that how Mum trains my brother and I, is how it should be with everyone. I now know that not everyone will like you, no matter how much you try to make peace. The chaperones were lovely and patient although I had my favourites. One of the Lion king chaperone- Neisha spoke life into my future and said to me "I want to see you in another show", which she did!!

Before my first contract finished, I was told that they would renew it for another six months. That was such great news! By this time I had kids waiting for me at the back door to let me know how much they enjoyed themselves. I was shy and most of the times did not know what to say. I guess I just did not get how huge of an opportunity I had. Somehow it was good because I felt normal and not better than others. I was the only one that remained in the show into the next contract. I was surprised, I had to pinch myself. I thought being in the show was a one off chance I was going to get. Well, I was wrong I remained on the show for a year and a half until I grew too tall to be little Simba. I met such great men and women during this time.

Matilda the musical

I was then called to audition for Matilda the musical as Nigel, and the theatre was a few minutes away from Lyceum theatre where the Lion king is. As a family, we have watched Matilda the movie a lot of times and I was so excited that I could not sleep early but to read my lines to everyone. I am sure everyone had enough, but not my brother Darmani. He loved it so much that he learnt the lines. The whole house turned into a theatre and at times we had to be stopped from jumping on the beds. The neighbors definitely noticed as they had watched me in Lion king. The day of the auditions was similar to that of Lion King in terms of number of kids and excitement but I felt more nervous. We had prayed the night before and Mum said what she would always say "well Denzel, you have worked hard to learn those lines. We leave it with God who knows more than our little minds and sees beyond what we are able to see." There were so many kids and I wondered for a moment if I was that special to make it this time. I told no one about my thoughts I just went in and gave it my very best and yes! I made it into the show as Nigel. We rehearsed for three months and we had the toughest dance teacher but he was the best. It was quite involving and we used a lot of energy. The first Matilda show was one I will always remember. I loved it and it was not as much work and scary as others said it was. The only issue was that I ate a lot of food afterwards. When my family was in the audience, I sometimes wanted to see them, but I had to concentrate and make them proud. A theatre that big, I could not always see them, but the squeezy hugs afterwards made me feel so loved. My younger brother Darmani has always enjoyed the shows and would always sing along or ask me to sing, which I did not always do. He would sulk if I did not, that is how much he enjoyed them.

My second contract was renewed as Bruce. Wow! I could eat the chocolate cake. The email for the third contract came like this; *we don't normally do this but we would like Denzel to continue the third round as Bruce. Will he accept this?*

Of course I said yes. That's when Mum reminded me that God does abundantly more than we could ever imagine. I loved it when my family and friends came to watch and to top it all; I was the face of Cambridge theatre. I loved walking past the poster and my Mum would pretend she was me by standing next to the poster and opening her mouth so wide! What an embarrassment!   Playing the part of Bruce was a bit more involving than being young Simba. I had to jump on desks. Mum was studying Human Nutrition by this time so she'd always remind me to eat well. She gave me extra milk to strengthen my bones as I would be jumping on desks. Sometimes when I got home, it was hilarious to find Mum with a warm glass of milk in her hand as soon as we opened the door. She seemed like a timed robot. Dad on the other hand would be calling me upstairs to my room just in case I was thinking of tiptoeing into the living room just to have a glimpse of the Television.

One of the best part in Matilda was when the music director helped me create my own riff which was the highest vocal tune that I sang during the show after I ate the cake. If you haven't heard it, goggle; surprise surprise Matilda. I even had an opportunity to perform on ITV.

I ate a lot during this period but Mum always made sure I did not eat junk. A small container of fruits, a big bottle of water and yoghurt was packed for me. Sometimes she would pack home cooked food in a warmer and I ate on the train. I did not have to buy junk as I had no excuse; she really made sure of it. After the performances, some people would come up to me to tell me how much they enjoyed the show. This reminded me that what I do is for the people and not for me or fame. I hoped that if someone comes into the theatre sad, they would leave smiling. One of my best days was when grandma came all the way from Malawi, Africa and watched my final show in Matilda. She said she was so proud of me.

Bugsy Malone musical

This was another special moment as I was called to audition before the open auditions. I couldn't get the American accent so I got offered the part of Fizzy for 6 months. I loved singing tomorrow. I had a chaperone that was so laid back and she gave us sweets. She was also a great singer. We met lovely people and Mum is still friends with some mums.

School of Rock musical

Towards the end of Bugsy Malone I auditioned for School of Rock. I went for endless auditions for this and I didn't think I would make it when I was measured and they said;"you are over five foot tall" (you have to be five foot or below to be in the show). I said to Mum; "we leave it in God's hands". I got the role. God made a way again and I was cast as James. I didn't do much but Mum said it's good not to get main parts at times so that I can learn that it's okay to be in the back roll at times. She never wants my talent to define me.

Not forgetting God's kingdom

With all the shows and private tuition, Mum had to rearrange schedules for me to go to church and sometimes I would go with my Aunt Rachel, but Dad would pick me up afterwards. I love church and even when I just stayed during the time we sang worship songs, it was a great experience. I did not go to many youth conferences but the few I went to were life impacting. They always told us to do something that makes a difference. That when we become successful, we should remember that it is not us alone lest we let others worship us, but that it is the Lord who gives us power to get wealth according to Deutronomy 8 verse 18. I also love the leaders and other kids. Everyone is so relaxed that I feel relaxed to be myself. I now belong to young adults group but was in a younger group before, called voltage and the girls and boys who taught and looked after us have been such a great support. Since I started acting in local theatres, they would come to watch my brother and I performing the Academy plays. My youth pastor even came to watch me in Matilda. He is so cool.

Stealing my limelight

Yes my younger brother, Darmani joined the Academy too. He somehow took the limelight as he is not as shy as I am. A lot of people used to come to me to say how adorable my brother is. I was kind of jealous sometimes but always remembered Mum and Dad's words that "each one of us is God's beloved, and He is so obsessed with us. His thoughts are precious". I would then smile and allow Darmani be adored, knowing that I too am adored.

Challenges

I haven't been in this industry that long but I've lost count of the auditions that I have been to. I could guess that it's about 50 and I haven't made it on so many occasions. I also did my 11 plus preparation mostly on the train before performances in Lion king. I have missed out on nice school trips and I haven't had a birthday party for 5 years because it's either am in rehearsals or performing. I have been on holiday with my family once in 4 years and this was before my last contract in Matilda.

After the musicals

I am now 13 years old and I finished School of Rock in February 2017. I have had a good rest and even celebrated my birthday with a party. I haven't been able to do this in 5 years. I have gone for endless auditions which I wasn't cast but my biggest disappointment was when I didn't get into the 4 o'clock club show on CBBC. I was so sad but Mum said, "at times steps are needed to get to a certain destination. If you get to the top too quickly you might not be able to stay there".

Money

One thing I have learnt is to save money. During each contract, my parents did not watch me so many times. Actually, my Dad wanted to save all the money that he regrets not watching me as much as Mum did. I was only allowed to spend so I could learn how to look for deals but not to finish all the money I made. I even tithed. Mum's advice was; when a contract is finished, don't just have loads of trainers, pictures and memories. Have some money in your account. Thankfully I listened and now I am still able to withdraw money (a little!!).

What next?

As the book is being published, I've been cast for my first ever filming role to record an educational video. This is a new platform and I am very excited. I wonder how many times the cameras roll for a video to be complete.

Do I know what the future holds? No!!! But I know the one who does which is God. He has been faithful and because he never changes, I believe he has a good plan for my future.

I am thankful

When I think of all the people that have contributed to me being in the West end theatres, I then remember my Aunt Rachel who chats a lot but sometimes gets serious. She would always say "there are people on your path that impact you in a great way and yet may never know, I pray they know so that they can live with a purpose and help others realize their dream and what they were born to do." She is right. Claire has been one of those people as well as Alex my previous agent not forgetting the Academy teachers. Of course there have been others that I probably would never meet and know who spoke well of me so that my contracts would be renewed. I will always be so grateful of these people and I hope I do the same for others.

I am now beginning to understand that I am surrounded by great people who help us in different ways. Mum shares Academy pickups with Aunt Phina who always turns up on time and she is lovely. I like getting into her car because she lets me sit in the front. Theatre mums always made me smile and my family is amazing. Dad never complains and he takes me to most auditions. Mum prays a lot and makes sure I eat well, stay humble and talks to me a lot as well as pick me up from performances. She doesn't like auditions. My brother helps me learn my lines. Aunt Rachel prays for me and keeps me grounded. My grandparents are always cheering me on. My granddad Verson Idi was my main Editor. He corrected me a lot!!!

My Academy family has been so supportive and they have watched me in each show! I don't take that for granted. I love you all.

There are so many people I haven't mentioned, mostly the kids I have performed with. They all have a special place in my heart.

The end

23

24

12081093R00016

Printed in Great Britain
by Amazon